W9-BRZ-690

Explorers & Exploration

The Travels of Francisco Pizarro

By Lara Bergen

Illustrated by Patrick O'Brien

Raintree Steck-Vaughn Publishers

A Harcourt Company

Austin • New York

www.steck-vaughn.com

Published by Raintree Steck-Vaughn Publishers,
an imprint of Steck-Vaughn Company

Library of Congress Cataloging-in-Publication Data
Bergen, Lara Rice.
Francisco Pizarro/by Lara Bergen
p. cm. — (Explorers and exploration)
Includes Index.
Summary: The life and conquests of the Spanish explorer who joined an expedition to the New World in 1502 and subsequently claimed for Spain parts of Mexico, Central America, and South America including Peru.
ISBN 0-7398-1489-3
1. Pizarro, Francisco, ca. 1475–1541—Juvenile literature
2. Peru—History—Conquest, 1522–1548—Juvenile literature
3. Governors—Peru—Biography—Juvenile literature
4. Explorers—Peru—Biography—Juvenile literature
5. Explorers—Spain—Biography—Juvenile literature
[1. Pizarro, Francisco, ca. 1475–1541. 2. Peru—History—Conquest, 1522–1548. 3. Explorers.]
I. Title. II. Series.

F3442.P776 B46 2000
985'.02'092—dc21 99-056144

Printed in the United States of America
10 9 8 7 6 5 4 3 2 1 LB 02 01 00

Illustration Acknowledgments
pp 5, 23, 25, 31, 32, and 39, John Blazejewski; pp 6, 19, 28, 35, New York Public Library Picture Collection; p 14, Department of Library Services, American Museum of Natural History. All other artwork is by Patrick O'Brien

Contents

A Land of Golden Treasure

Francisco Pizarro was born around 1470 in Trujillo, Spain. At that time Europeans did not know what was across the Atlantic Ocean. They were not even sure there was land on the other side. There were tales of strange people and fortunes to be made. But who had the courage—and the money—to go sailing off into the unknown?

Such an idea was far from Pizarro's mind when he was young. Francisco grew up very poor. His father was an officer in the Spanish army, and his mother came from a poor family. Pizarro and his brothers never learned to read or write—and never would. As boys, they worked on pig farms for money and food.

Still Pizarro began to dream of fame and fortune. When he was a teenager, he joined the Spanish army. He was a fine soldier. Then, in 1492, something happened that would change his life. Christopher Columbus sailed across the Atlantic Ocean and returned to the King and Queen of Spain with unusual plants and people—and gold! There was more where that came from. Columbus had reached the West Indies.

Francisco Pizarro

Over the next few years, Pizarro took part in many Spanish army campaigns, or actions. With his fellow conquistadors, he helped claim more of what is now Mexico, Colombia, and Panama for Spain. And in 1513 Pizarro helped Vasco Núñez de Balboa cross the Isthmus of Panama. This is the narrow strip of land that connects the continents of North and South America.

It was the first time that Europeans had reached the "Great South Sea," or Pacific Ocean, by land. It was also the first time Pizarro heard tales of a great land to the south. In this land, the native people said, strange sheep were on the mountains. People drank from golden cups and ate from golden dishes. The native people called the kingdom Biru. But the Spanish did not understand the word. From then on, they would call the land Peru.

Stories of long-necked sheep and jewels led Pizarro to the kingdom the native people called Biru.

Still Pizarro began to dream of fame and fortune. When he was a teenager, he joined the Spanish army. He was a fine soldier. Then, in 1492, something happened that would change his life. Christopher Columbus sailed across the Atlantic Ocean and returned to the King and Queen of Spain with unusual plants and people—and gold! There was more where that came from. Columbus had reached the West Indies.

Francisco Pizarro

After that, many explorers sailed from Spain to the Americas in search of fortune for themselves and their rulers. By the early 1500s, Spain had one of the best navies in the world. And Spain had claimed part of the Americas—what we now call the islands of the Caribbean Sea and Central America—for themselves. But these lands already belonged to native peoples.

The Spaniards did not care. To them, those people were "savages," because they did not live the way the Spaniards did. And they did not believe in the same God. The Spaniards thought they should bring their God and their government to the native peoples. In return, the Spaniards took the native people's land and their gold. They killed them if they did not do what the Spanish said. These Spanish conquerors were known as conquistadors.

In 1502, Pizarro decided that he was also meant to be a conquistador. He left the army and joined an expedition. This group was going to the new Spanish colony on the island of Hispaniola (now Haiti and the Dominican Republic).

Conquistadors

Over the next few years, Pizarro took part in many Spanish army campaigns, or actions. With his fellow conquistadors, he helped claim more of what is now Mexico, Colombia, and Panama for Spain. And in 1513 Pizarro helped Vasco Núñez de Balboa cross the Isthmus of Panama. This is the narrow strip of land that connects the continents of North and South America.

It was the first time that Europeans had reached the "Great South Sea," or Pacific Ocean, by land. It was also the first time Pizarro heard tales of a great land to the south. In this land, the native people said, strange sheep were on the mountains. People drank from golden cups and ate from golden dishes. The native people called the kingdom Biru. But the Spanish did not understand the word. From then on, they would call the land Peru.

Stories of long-necked sheep and jewels led Pizarro to the kingdom the native people called Biru.

From the moment Pizarro heard the stories of this strange land, he dreamed of finding it. He dreamed of conquering it, or winning it by force. Like all conquistadors, Pizarro wanted to add new lands to the Spanish Empire and bring Christianity to the native peoples. He also hoped to claim glory—and gold—for himself. Still, it would be several years before this dream could come true.

The conquistadors set out to bring Christianity to new lands.

A Line in the Sand

In honor of his service to his country, the Spanish ruler made Pizarro mayor of Panama in 1519. Over the next few years, Pizarro grew rich. Still this was not enough for him. He knew that greater riches and power lay to the south. And in 1523, when he was close to 50 years old, Pizarro decided it was time to find Peru.

Of course, conquering a kingdom would not be easy. So Pizarro turned to two friends to help him. The first, Diego de Almagro, was a brave and popular soldier. Pizarro knew Almagro could help him lead an army across South America. The other friend was a wealthy priest named Fernando de Luque. De Luque would pay for the expedition. The three men agreed that they would work together. If they found any fortune, they would split it three ways after giving a share to the ruler of Spain.

THREE OF FRANCISCO PIZARRO'S VOYAGES

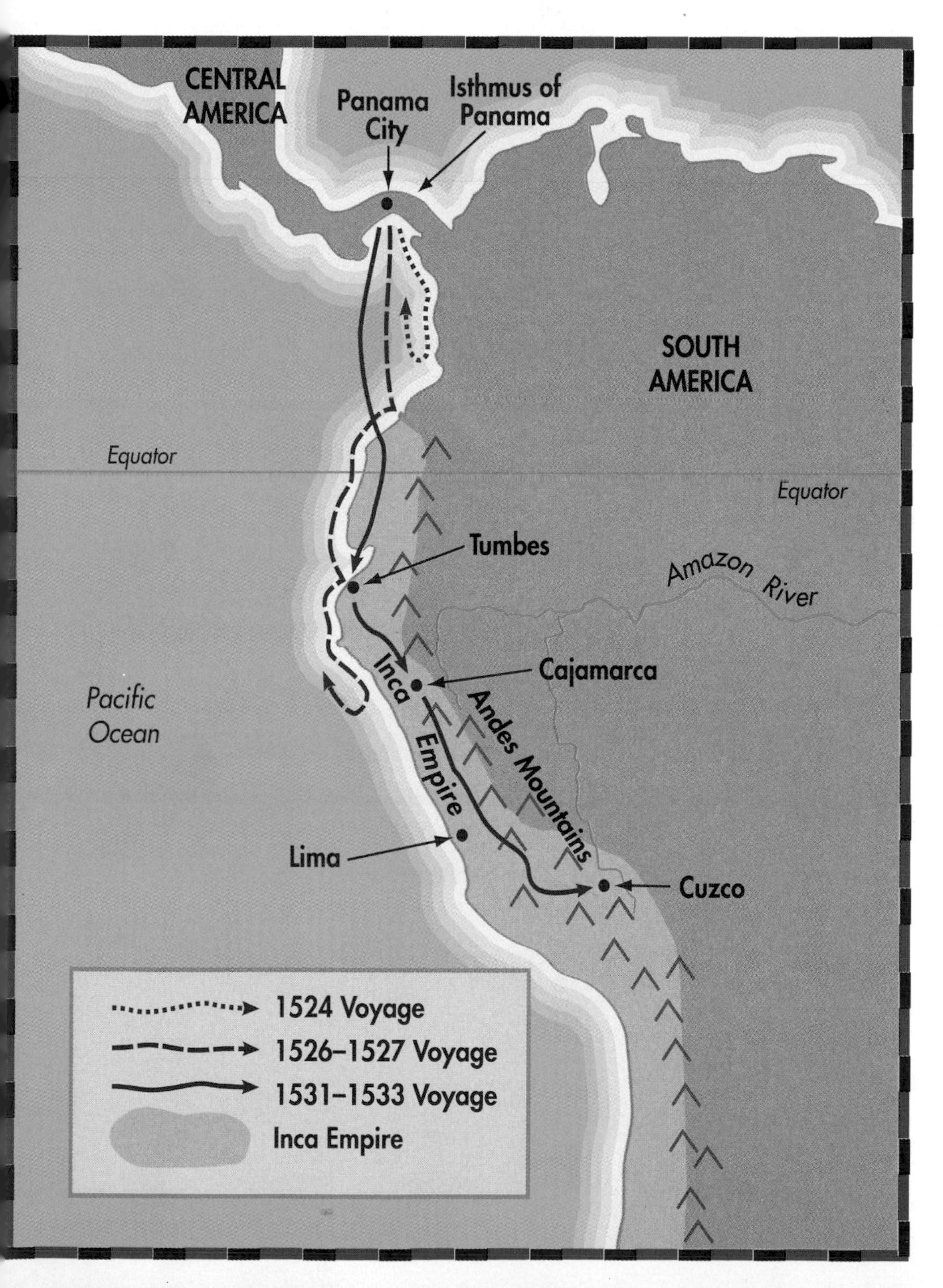

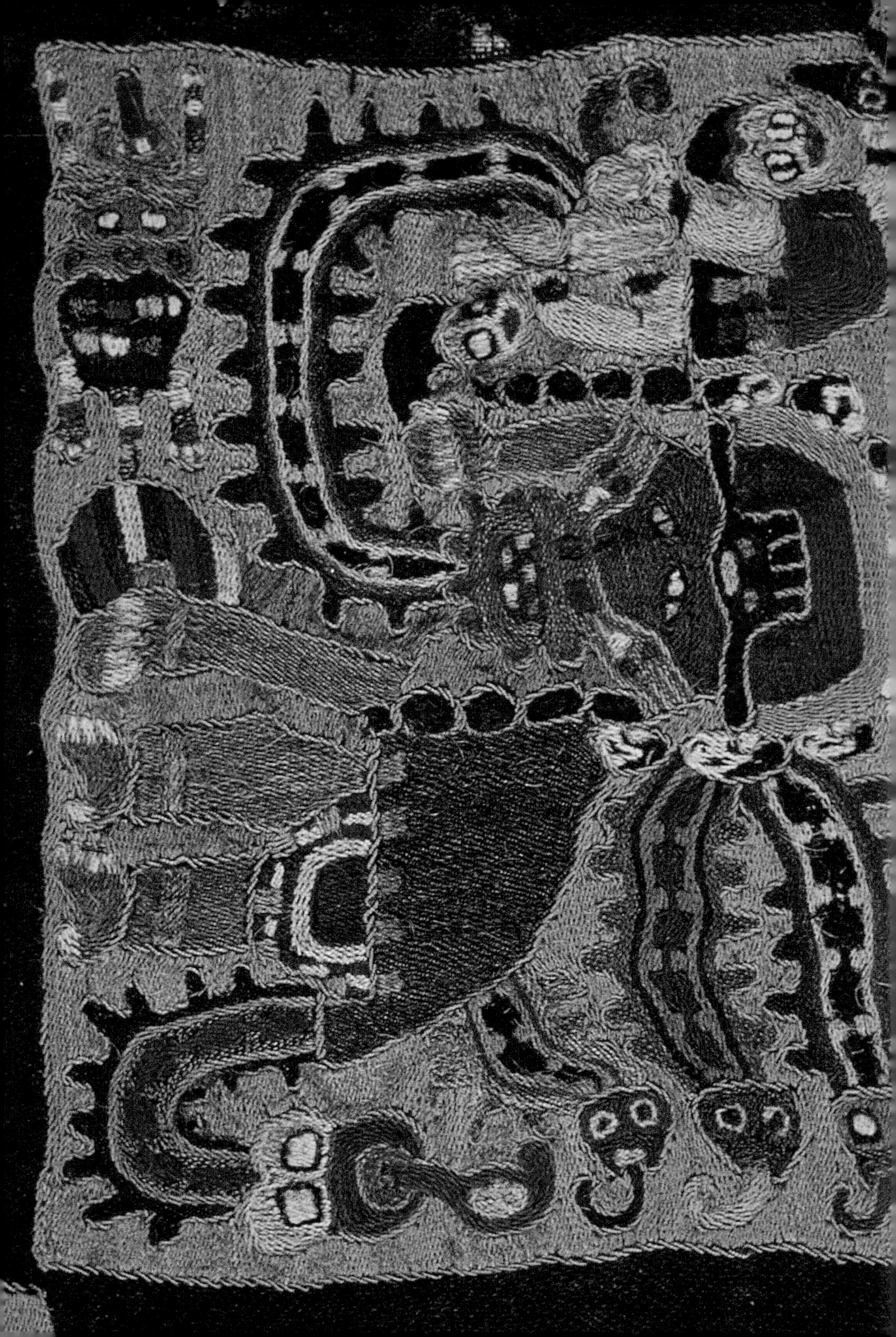

In 1524, after a year of preparation, Pizarro sailed south from Panama with more than 100 soldiers and many horses. Almagro was to follow later with more men. Bad weather slowed Pizarro's ships. Pizarro and his men decided to leave their ships and go on by land. But the coast of Peru was no easier. The men wanted to turn back. They were tired and nearly starving. But Pizarro made them keep going. He reminded them of the gold they were going to find. They finally found some native people, and signs of gold, but more than 20 soldiers died. Some starved or died of disease. Some were killed by the native people.

The native people whom the Spaniards came upon were the Inca. They were not the only native people in the region. But they were by far the largest and most powerful group. Since the 1400s they had ruled an empire about 250 miles (400 km) wide and 2,500 miles (4,000 km) long. They called this empire Tahuantinsuya, or "Kingdom of the Four Quarters." It was about twice as big as Spain. The land covered not only the country that is Peru today, but also Ecuador, Chile, and parts of Bolivia and Argentina. The Four Quarters included more than ten million people.

The Inca wove beautiful cloths.

To the Inca, gold was a part of life. Like many ancient people, the Inca worshiped the sun. They had several gods, but they considered the sun their father. The sun's wife, the moon, was their mother. Gold, it was said, was the sweat of the sun. Silver was the tears of his wife, the moon.

The Inca's ruler, called the Sapa Inca, was believed to come directly from the sun god. He was thought to have the powers of a god. He lived with his wives and children in the capital city, Cuzco.

The Inca had no written language. However, they did keep records with long knotted strings called quipus. They built miles of roads, bridges, and great cities. Messengers traveled between cities, bringing news and messages to the people. This helped link the different cities together. The Inca built farms on the sides of mountains and stored food in case crops failed. They wove beautiful, colorful cloth. But what the Spaniards noticed most of all was their large supply of gold, silver, and emeralds.

The Inca wondered whether the white men with beards, armor, guns, and fast horses were gods. Even if they were, the Inca fought the Spanish because they were afraid of the strangers.

When Almagro finally caught up with Pizarro, his army also showed scars of battle with the Inca. Almagro had even lost the sight in one eye.

Pizarro and Almagro agreed they would need even more men and supplies. How else could they conquer such a mighty people? So they returned to Panama.

In 1526 Pizarro and Almagro set off again for the south with several ships and almost 200 men. This journey was also hard, but it was even more rewarding. By following the Inca's paved roads once they landed, the conquistadors found villages filled with gold cups and platters. They also found thousands of Inca soldiers.

In order to conquer this rich and powerful empire, Pizarro would need many more men. Some of his own men were not sure that this would help. They did not feel that gold was worth their lives. They wanted to go back to Panama.

Pizarro decided to send Almagro back to Panama with the gold that they had found. Almagro would get as many new soldiers as he could. And he would take the soldiers who did not want to stay in Peru with him.

When Almagro arrived in Panama, however, he found a new governor had taken over. This governor did not believe in Pizarro's expedition. He believed the soldiers who told him that fighting the Inca was a big mistake. Instead of letting more men go back with Almagro, he sent Almagro south with empty ships.

Almagro also had orders to bring the men who were still in Peru back to Panama. He also had a message for Pizarro. Pizarro could go ahead with his voyage if he wanted to. But it would be without help from the government.

Pizarro was angry when he heard this. He drew his sword from his belt and drew a line in the sand. On one side, he told his men, "lies Peru and its riches." On the other side, "Panama and its poverty. Choose, conquistadors," he cried. Then he jumped across the line.

The choice was not an easy one for Pizarro's men. After all, some of their fellow soldiers had already died looking for riches. Pizarro waited. In the end, only 13 soldiers jumped over the line with him.

Pizarro asked his men to choose poverty or riches.

By Order of the Emperor

When the governor heard of Pizarro's action, he was won over. While Pizarro and his followers waited months in Peru, the governor let Almagro go back with one ship and new soldiers, but only for six months.

Together again, Pizarro and Almagro sailed even farther south with their small group. At last they reached the large Inca city of Tumbes. They were amazed by the wealth of this great city, as well as by its size.

Pizarro quickly learned that taking gold by force would not work there. The city was too big and his group was too small. So Pizarro pretended to be a friend instead. He gave gifts to the chief of Tumbes. And when the chief offered him gifts of gold in return, Pizarro agreed to take just a few jars of gold and silver and three native men.

Pizarro and his small group sailed farther south toward the Inca city of Tumbes.

With these treasures and men, Pizarro sailed a few miles farther south. Then, finding no more cities, he returned to Panama. Pizarro hoped that the gold from Tumbes would change the governor's mind about Peru. But the governor stood firm. There would be no more trips south. So Pizarro, Almagro, and de Luque decided to try a different approach. Pizarro would sail to Spain and appeal to the emperor himself.

In 1528 Pizarro appeared at the court of Charles V with emeralds and the skin of one of the Inca's "long-necked sheep." This is what we now know as a llama. He described the millions of native people waiting to learn about Christianity. And he told of millions of tons of gold waiting to be sent back to Spain.

King Charles was won over. He gave Pizarro the title of Governor and Captain General of the Colony of Peru. Pizarro also received a large salary and was told to conquer the territory for Spain. Pizarro prepared to return to Panama. But first he stopped in his hometown. There he talked four of his half brothers—Gonzalo, Juan, Martin, and Hernando—and a cousin, Pedro, into going with him. On January 19, 1530, the Pizarros set sail for the Americas.

Pizarro appears before King Charles V in 1528.

When Pizarro arrived in Panama, Almagro and de Luque were happy to hear that Charles V had supported them. But they were not happy to learn of Pizarro's new title and salary. Almagro had only been made governor of the city of Tumbes. And de Luque was made Bishop. To make them feel better, Pizarro promised them that they would still each get equal shares when they conquered Peru. And in 1531, the expedition set off from Panama once again.

Two weeks later Pizarro's three ships landed in a bay north of Tumbes. While the ships sailed back to Panama for more men and supplies, the conquistadors took off on foot through the country. They stole riches from every small village they came across. Then they met up with their ships again in another bay farther south and sailed on to Tumbes.

When Pizarro's troops landed in Tumbes, however, they were surprised to find that there was little gold left. Much of it had been taken during an Inca civil war. Just a year after Pizarro's last visit, the Inca leader, or Sapa Inca, Huayna Capac, had died. Huascar, his oldest son, had been named the new Sapa Inca. But another son, Atahualpa, wanted to be ruler. The result was a long war that left Huascar in prison and Atahualpa in control. The Inca Empire was then very weak.

Atahualpa

Pizarro was pleased. The Inca Empire was divided. Its armies were tired, and the people were confused. It was the perfect time to conquer them! All Pizarro had to do was capture the new leader.

As soon as he could, Pizarro set off for the city of Cajamarca. There, he was told, Atahualpa and his army were camped. To get there, though, Pizarro's army would have to cross one of the world's highest mountain ranges, the Andes.

The Sun King Falls

The conquistadors gave the mountains the name Andes after the Inca word *andenes.* This meant hillside farm terraces. But the Andes were much more than hills. Covered with ice and snow, and with steep ledges, these mountains were deadly. It took the conquistadors seven days to cross them.

On the other side of the mountain, Pizarro saw a valley filled with farms. In the middle was the city of Cajamarca. And across the valley there were tents as far as the conquistadors could see. It was the camp of Atahualpa and about 50,000 of his soldiers. Pizarro had fewer than 200 men.

Pizarro neared the town. Messengers went back and forth between the small Spanish army and the great Inca army. Pizarro tried to arrange a peaceful meeting with Atahualpa. His real plan, though, was to capture the ruler—and with him, Peru.

Pizarro's army marched into Cajamarca with waving flags, loud trumpets, and shining armor. They were surprised to find the town completely empty.

Pizarro sent Hernando de Soto to Atahualpa's camp to talk to him. When the Spaniards finally found the ruler, he was bathing in a spring, surrounded by many chiefs and many wives.

The Sapa Inca had not been frightened by the Spanish army because of its small number. But he was interested when he saw the men's armor and horses. He told the Spaniards he would meet Pizarro in the city the next day.

As soon as Pizarro heard this, he gathered his men together to pray for success. Then he began to set his trap.

Pizarro approaching Cajamarca

The next day Pizarro had his men hide around the town's central plaza. This was an open square where the people gathered. Then they waited for Atahualpa. He arrived outside the city just before sunset. But he sent a messenger to say he would not enter it until morning.

Pizarro was furious. His trap was ready, and he would not wait any longer. He sent a message back to Atahualpa. He told the ruler that a great feast had been planned in his honor, even though it wasn't true. The lie worked. Atahualpa did not want to disappoint his visitors. He agreed to enter the city that day.

The way Atahualpa arrived was like nothing the Spaniards had ever seen. First there were singers and servants in bright colors. They swept the streets with palm leaves. Then there came many soldiers dressed in bright cotton tunics and carrying no arms.

Atahualpa was carried into the town plaza on a pure gold throne, surrounded by guards dressed in gold and silver. On his head he wore a crown of tall black and white feathers. Around his neck was a collar of emeralds. When he looked around and saw no Spaniards in sight, the great Sapa Inca was not surprised. He guessed that the strangers were too awed and afraid of him to show their faces.

A priest blessing the Inca

Pizarro let Atahualpa wait for a few minutes. Then he sent out a priest, Friar Vicente de Valverde, and a native translator named Felippo. The priest held up a wooden cross and a Bible. He explained to Atahualpa that the great Spanish ruler, Charles V, had sent Pizarro to rule the Inca and make them Christians. Then he handed the Sapa Inca the Bible. Proudly Atahualpa replied that his people did not need a new ruler or a new religion. He pointed toward the setting sun. "My god still lives in the heaven and looks down on his children," he told the priest.

Friar Valverde telling Atahualpa about Christianity

Pizarro was not surprised. As planned, he waved a white handkerchief, and his army came out of hiding. Cannons roared, firing into crowds. On horseback and on foot, the Spaniards killed as many Inca soldiers as they could. Then they chased the ones who tried to run away. In a matter of minutes, thousands of Inca were killed. And Atahualpa was taken prisoner.

The Beginning of Peru

The next day Pizarro's soldiers rode into the Inca army camp. They told the soldiers there of Atahualpa's capture and took all the gold they could find. Then they went back to Cajamarca and hunted for more.

In the city, Pizarro kept Atahualpa locked in a room. But he still treated the Sapa Inca like a king. He gave Atahualpa the best food and allowed him to have visitors. Atahualpa even learned Spanish and how to play chess with the conquistadors. He also learned that what the conquistadors wanted most was gold.

Atahualpa made Pizarro an offer. In exchange for his freedom, he would give Pizarro enough gold to fill his cell. And he would give enough silver to fill it twice! Naturally, Pizarro accepted.

For the next nine months, treasure from around the Inca Empire flowed into Cajamarca. There was so much treasure, it was said, the Spanish soldiers began to make horseshoes out of silver.

As Atahualpa waited for his freedom, he also thought about his brother, Huascar, still in prison. Fearing that Huascar might use this chance to gain the upper hand, Atahualpa sent out an order for his execution.

Meanwhile, Pizarro had begun to worry that three rooms full of gold and silver were still not enough. So he sent soldiers south, to the great Inca capital, Cuzco. They were to take what they could from there. The Inca people did not try to stop them. Without a ruler to tell them what to do, they waited and did nothing.

Pizarro also worried about keeping his promise. If he freed Atahualpa, the Sapa Inca might order his ten million subjects to attack the Spanish.

Pizarro's men conquering Atahualpa

If they attacked, Pizarro's small army would never stand a chance. And so, in the summer of 1533, Pizarro decided to put Atahualpa on trial.

Inca gold in the form of a helmet and small statues

Atahualpa was accused of having his brother killed, which was true. He was also accused of plotting to overthrow the Spanish army, which was not. Pizarro and Almagro quickly found Atahualpa guilty and sentenced him to death.

Atahualpa's death left his people without a ruler. But it did not keep them from finally rising against the Spaniards. They also buried or hid all the gold that they had left. To try to gain control, Pizarro had thousands more Inca killed. Those he did not kill, he made slaves and forced them to look for gold and silver. At the same time, he sent Almagro south to take over the part of the Inca Empire that is now Chile. He sent another conquistador, Sebastián de Belalcázar, north to conquer what is now Ecuador.

Pizarro's Peru, however, was still out of control. So he tried another plan. He named his own Sapa Inca. For ruler he chose Atahualpa and Huascar's younger brother, Manco. Manco was one of the few Inca who seemed friendly. Pizarro believed Manco would do anything he told him to do. For a while Manco did.

But in 1535, Manco took a chance. Pizarro had left Cuzco to build a new capital. It was Ciudad de los Reyes, or "City of Kings." This is the city that is now Lima, Peru. While Pizarro was gone, Manco used the Spaniards' own arms and horses to try to take over Cuzco. He almost succeeded. But in the end the Spanish were too strong. Manco was forced to give up and hide in the mountains.

This was not the end of Pizarro's troubles, though. Soon after, Almagro returned to Cuzco from Chile—angry and bitter. He had not found the treasure in Chile he had hoped to find. Instead, his so-called partner, Pizarro, had ended up with all the wealth and power.

Disappointed, Almagro took Pizarro's brother Hernando prisoner. Almagro told Pizarro that he would only let Hernando go if Almagro could control the rich city of Cuzco. Pizarro let Almagro think he had agreed—but only until he knew his brother was safe. As soon as Hernando was released, Pizarro sent soldiers to Cuzco to kill Almagro and take back the city.

The Inca city of Cuzco, Peru

For three years Pizarro ruled the rich new colony of Peru. But on June 26, 1541, Almagro's followers finally took revenge. Pizarro was just sitting down to lunch in his grand new palace in Lima. A group of men stormed into the dining room and attacked him with swords. Pizarro had no chance to defend himself.

In a strange twist of fate, Pizarro was murdered by fellow Spaniards whom he had plotted against, not the people from whom he'd stolen a nation.

Pizarro was killed by Almagro's followers in 1541.

This was not, of course, the end for Spain. It was just the beginning. Within 50 years, the great Inca Empire was destroyed by war and disease, both of which the Spaniards had brought. The land was divided by Spain into the nations of Ecuador, Bolivia, Chile, and Peru. The continent of South America was changed forever. Ancient villages and temples were destroyed. Native peoples were forced to change their religion and their way of life. All these changes helped make Spain one of the richest and most powerful empires for many years.

Other Events of the 16th Century
(1501 – 1600)

During the century that Pizarro was exploring South America, events were happening in other parts of the world. Some of these were:

1500s European traders visit China.

1502 Portuguese navigator Vasco da Gama makes his second voyage to India in order to expand trade.

1520 Ferdinand Magellan, the Portuguese navigator, sails around the southern tip of South America.

1521 Hernán Cortés, a Spanish conquistador, conquers the Aztec empire in Mexico.

1524 Giovanni da Verrazano, an Italian sailor, explores the coast of North America from North Carolina to Maine.

1543 Portuguese sailors are the first Europeans to reach Japan.

1546 Destruction of the Mali empire in Africa by Songhay.

1571 Portuguese create African colony in Angola.

Time Line

c. 1200	Inca Empire is founded in the Cuzco Valley.
c. 1475	Pizarro is born in Trujillo, Spain.
1488	Bartholomeu Dias rounds the Cape of Good Hope.
1492	Christopher Columbus crosses the Atlantic Ocean and reaches the West Indies.
1498	Columbus reaches South America.
1513	Vasco Núñez de Balboa crosses the Isthmus of Panama with Pizarro and reaches the Pacific Ocean.
1518–1521	Hernán Cortés takes over Mexico from the Aztecs.
1522	Ferdinand Magellan's expedition goes around the world.
1524	Pizarro first sails to South America.

1526	Pizarro sails to South America for a second time.
1528	Pizarro sails to Spain to ask for Charles V's support.
1528	Inca civil war breaks out between Huascar and Atahualpa.
1532 (November)	Pizarro crosses the Andes and captures Atahualpa.
1533 (August)	Pizarro orders the death of Atahualpa.
1533 (November)	Pizarro captures Inca capital, Cuzco, and takes over the Inca Empire.
1533 (December)	Pizarro crowns Manco as Sapa Inca.
1535 (January)	Pizarro founds Lima, Peru.
1535	Manco tries to take back Cuzco.
1538 (July)	Pizarro orders Almagro's death.
1541 (June 26)	Pizarro is murdered by Almagro's followers.
1544	Viceroyalty of Peru is formally set up by Spain.

Glossary

Andes (AN-deez) A major mountain range running north to south along the west coast of South America

bay (BAY) A part of the ocean that is partly enclosed by land

campaign (cam-PAIN) An army action

civil war (SIV-ul) A war between people living in the same country

conquistador (kon-KEES-tuh-dor) A "conqueror," or leader in the Spanish conquest of North and South America in the 1500s

continent (KON-tuh-nent) One of the earth's seven great landmasses (North America, South America, Africa, Asia, Europe, Australia, Antarctica)

emperor (EM-pur-ur) The ruler of a large territory

empire (EM-pir) A large territory that is under the rule of one leader

execution (ek-sih-KYU-shun) Putting to death

expedition (ek-spuh-DISH-un) A trip for a special purpose, such as to explore or take over lands

Hispaniola (his-pan-YO-luh) Island in the Caribbean; today Haiti and the Dominican Republic

Inca (EEN-kuh) The native ruling empire of the area that is today Peru from about 1200 until the Spanish conquest

isthmus (IS-mus) A narrow strip of land with water on both sides, connecting two larger areas of land

llama (LAH-muh) Woolly South American pack animal; related to the camel, but smaller and without a hump

poverty (POHV-urt-ee) Lacking enough money or goods

quipu (KEY-poo) Knotted string used by the Inca for keeping records

Sapa Inca (SAH-pah EEN-kah) Native ruler of the Inca Empire

terrace (TER-us) A level ridge made in a hillside on which to grow crops

translator (trans-LAYT-ur) A person who turns one language into another so it can be understood

Index